OUR Values

SHARING OUR GLOBAL COMMUNITY

By Steffi Cavell-Clarke

Crabtree Publishing Company
www.crabtreebooks.com
1-800-387-7650

Published in Canada
Crabtree Publishing
616 Welland Avenue
St. Catharines, ON
L2M 5V6

Published in the United States
Crabtree Publishing
PMB 59051
350 Fifth Ave, 59th Floor
New York, NY 10118

Published by Crabtree Publishing Company in 2017

First Published by Book Life in 2016
Copyright © 2017 Book Life

Author
Steffi Cavell-Clarke

Editors
Grace Jones
Janine Deschenes

Design
Natalie Carr

Proofreader
Crystal Sikkens

Production coordinator and
prepress technician (interior)
Margaret Amy Salter

Prepress technician (covers)
Ken Wright

Print coordinator
Katherine Berti

Photographs
Shutterstock: sunsinger: page 7 (top); Matej Kastelic:
        page 7 (bottom); Sergei Bachlakov: page 11;
        Dmitrydesign: page 14; Migel: page 17
Thinkstock: front cover
Other images by Shutterstock

Printed in Hong Kong/012017/BK20161024

Library and Archives Canada Cataloguing in Publication

Cavell-Clarke, Steffi, author
        Sharing our global community / Steffi Cavell-Clarke.

(Our values)
Issued in print and electronic formats.
ISBN 978-0-7787-3264-8 (hardback).--ISBN 978-0-7787-3330-0
(paperback).--ISBN 978-1-4271-1895-0 (html)

        1. Communities--Juvenile literature. 2. Community life--
Juvenile literature. 3. Social participation--Juvenile literature.
4. Political participation--Juvenile literature. I. Title.

HM756.C39 2016   j307   C2016-906661-4
                                            C2016-906662-2

Library of Congress Cataloging-in-Publication Data

CIP available at Library of Congress

CONTENTS

Words that are bolded, like **this**, can be found in the glossary on page 24.

WHAT ARE VALUES?

Values are the things that you believe are important, such as helping those who are in need. The way we think and behave depend on our values. Values teach us how we should **respect** each other and ourselves. Sharing values with others helps us work and live together in a **community**.

Respecting others

Making good choices

Understanding different beliefs

Working together with others

Values make our communities better places to live. Think about the values in your community. What is important to you and the people around you?

Helping others

Sharing your ideas

OUR COMMUNITY

A community is a group of people who live, work, and play in a place. Often, people in a community share similar attitudes and values. A person can be part of many different communities. Your school, neighborhood, and home are all part of your community.

Together, all people living on planet Earth belong to one big community—the global community. Within our global community, many other smaller communities can be found. Each and every community is important, whether it is a small village community or our global community.

A village community in Tulear, Madagascar

A city community in Tokyo, Japan

WHY ARE COMMUNITIES IMPORTANT?

Being part of a community allows us to make friends and work together to solve problems. Communities can also give us a sense of **belonging** and help us feel that we are accepted by others.

It is important that we care for other people in our community and help to keep each other safe.

Everyone in the world is part of one big community, so we should be kind and caring toward everyone.

DIFFERENT CULTURES

Culture is the ideas and behaviors of a group of people. Each community includes the culture or cultures of the people who live there. Every community should also welcome new and different cultures.

Different communities may have particular cultural **traditions** or hold special celebrations throughout the year. People in many different communities celebrate Chinese New Year. People can celebrate this **festival** in many ways, such as by wearing traditional clothing or by taking part in large street parades.

CULTURES IN OUR COMMUNITY

A community can have many people with different cultures. It can also include people of different **religions** and **nationalities**. This is called a **multicultural** community.

Our global community is a multicultural community because it includes all the people on Earth.

It is important that we always welcome people into our communities and accept their cultures, beliefs, and traditions, even if they are different from our own. Being part of a community means that you should accept everyone in it.

COMMUNITY HELPERS

There are people who live in our communities that have special jobs that make our communities better places to live. These people might help keep us safe, such as crossing guards, or help in other ways such as keeping parks clean or driving the bus that takes us to school.

Police officers, doctors, and firefighters are able to help us in an **emergency**. It is important that we respect the people who help us. We can show our respect for them by following the rules and listening when they tell us to do something.

LISTENING TO OTHERS

We all have the **freedom** to express our cultures in our communities. We expect others to accept our cultures, so it is important that we accept the cultures of others, too. We can do this by asking questions about others' cultures and listening to understand their beliefs and traditions.

Tina listened to Jasmine as she told their class about how she celebrates carnival every year with her family. Jasmine explained that carnival is a celebration that is part of her religion. Tina decided to attend carnival with Jasmine and her family so she could learn more about their culture.

The biggest carnival celebration is held in Rio de Janeiro, Brazil.

OUR COMMUNITY AT SCHOOL

You are not only a part of the community where you live, you are also a part of your school community. Your school community includes many people such as teachers, students, and volunteers. It is important that we respect others at school by listening and following the rules.

Marie and her friends saw that one of their classmates, Akira, looked sad. They asked her how she was feeling, and listened to her as she explained the reasons why she was upset. Marie asked Akira if she would like to join their game to cheer her up and show her that they care.

OUR COMMUNITY AT HOME

We often share the same cultures and communities with our families. Our family members can teach us a lot about the values of our culture and traditions.

Jessica goes to church every Sunday with her family. They meet other members of the community there. They sing and pray to God together. Jessica is free to celebrate her beliefs in her community.

MAKING A DIFFERENCE

It can be difficult for someone to move to a new community, so it is important that we welcome them. We can do this by saying hello and being friendly. We can also ask them about the community they came from. We should remember that, together, we all share a global community!

Remember to always tell your parent or the person who looks after you before speaking to a stranger.

We can make our community a better place to live by respecting the people and places in it. One way we can make a difference in our community is by helping the **environment**. We can do this by throwing our garbage in a trash can and reusing plastic shopping bags.

23

GLOSSARY

belonging [bih-LAWNG-ing] Being part of something
community [kuh-MYOO-ni-tee] A group of people who live, work, and play in a place
emergency [ih-MUR-juh n-see] A dangerous problem that requires action
environment [en-VAHY-ruh n muh nt] Your surroundings
festival [FES-tuh-vuh l] A celebration that includes ceremonies or other events
freedom [FREE-duh m] Being allowed to do something
multicultural [muhl-tee-KUHL-cher-uh l] Describing a community that has many different cultures
nationality [nash-uh-NAL-i-tee] The status of belonging to a nation or country
religion [ri-LIJ-uh n] A set of values and beliefs that people follow
respect [ri-SPEKT] The act of giving something or someone the attention it deserves
traditions [truh-DISH-uh ns] Beliefs or practices that have been handed down over a long period of time

INDEX